HOMES OF THE
NATIVE AMERICANS

Colleen Madonna Flood Williams

MASON CREST
PHILADELPHIA

NATIVE AMERICAN LIFE

HOMES OF THE NATIVE AMERICANS

Colleen Madonna Flood Williams

SENIOR CONSULTING EDITOR DR. TROY JOHNSON
PROFESSOR OF HISTORY AND AMERICAN INDIAN STUDIES
CALIFORNIA STATE UNIVERSITY

MC MASON CREST
PHILADELPHIA

As always, to Paul R. Williams and Dillon J. Meehan
with all my love.
For Big D, Noreen, Patrick Jr., Dennis, and Daniel Flood
with love.

Mason Crest
450 Parkway Drive, Suite D
Broomall, PA 19008
www.masoncrest.com

Printed and bound in the United States of America.

CPSIA Compliance Information: Batch #NAR2013. For further information, contact Mason Crest at 1-866-MCP-Book

First printing
1 3 5 7 9 8 6 4 2

Library of Congress Cataloging-in-Publication Data

Williams, Colleen Madonna Flood.
  Homes of the native Americans / Colleen Madonna Flood Williams.
    pages cm. — (Native American life)
  Includes bibliographical references and index.
  ISBN 978-1-4222-2965-1 (hc)
  ISBN 978-1-4222-8852-8 (ebook)
  1. Indians of North America—Dwellings—Juvenile literature. I. Title.
  E98.D9W54 2013
  392.3'60899708—dc23
                                        2013007477

Native American Life series ISBN: 978-1-4222-2963-7

TABLE OF CONTENTS

INTRODUCTION

For hundreds of years the dominant image of the Native American has been that of a stoic warrior, often wearing a full-length eagle feather headdress, riding a horse in pursuit of the buffalo, or perhaps surrounding some unfortunate wagon train filled with innocent west-bound American settlers. Unfortunately there has been little written or made available to the general public to dispel this erroneous generalization. This misrepresentation has resulted in an image of native people that has been translated into books, movies, and television programs that have done little to look deeply into the native worldview, cosmology, and daily life. Not until the 1990 movie *Dances with Wolves* were native people portrayed as having a human persona. For the first time, native people could express humor, sorrow, love, hate, peace, and warfare. For the first time native people could express themselves in words other than "ugh" or "Yes, Kemo Sabe." This series has been written to provide a more accurate and encompassing journey into the world of the Native Americans.

When studying the native world of the Americas, it is extremely important to understand that there are few "universals" that apply across tribal boundaries. With over 500 nations and 300 language groups the worlds of the Native Americans were diverse. The traditions of one group may or may not have been shared by neighboring groups. Sports, games, dance, subsistence patterns, clothing, and religion differed—greatly in some instances. And although nearly all native groups observed festivals and ceremonies necessary to insure the renewal of their worlds, these too varied greatly.

Of equal importance to the breaking down of old myopic and stereotypic images is that the authors in this series credit Native

Americans with a sense of agency. Contrary to the views held by the Europeans who came to North and South America and established the United States, Canada, Mexico, and other nations, some Native American tribes had sophisticated political and governing structures—that of the member nations of the Iroquois League, for example. Europeans at first denied that native people had religions but rather "worshiped the devil," and demanded that Native Americans abandon their religions for the Christian worldview. The readers of this series will learn that native people had well-established religions, led by both men and women, long before the European invasion began in the 16th and 17th centuries.

Gender roles also come under scrutiny in this series. European settlers in the northeastern area of the present-day United States found it appalling that native women were "treated as drudges" and forced to do the men's work in the agricultural fields. They failed to understand, as the reader will see, that among this group the women owned the fields and scheduled the harvests. Europeans also failed to understand that Iroquois men were diplomats and controlled over one million square miles of fur-trapping area. While Iroquois men sat at the governing council, Iroquois clan matrons caucused with tribal members and told the men how to vote.

These are small examples of the material contained in this important series. The reader is encouraged to use the extended bibliographies provided with each book to expand his or her area of specific interest.

Dr. Troy Johnson
Professor of History and American Indian Studies
California State University

Representation of a Native American family at Russell Cave National Monument, a site in present-day Alabama that was apparently inhabited by Paleo-Indians some 10,000 years ago. Archaeologists believe that it was around this time that Native Americans began constructing their own dwellings and forming communities

1 The First Native American Homes

Where did the first Americans build their homes? Did they live in open camps, caves, or timber-and-earthen houses? **Archeologists** and **anthropologists** are still trying to answer these important questions.

For many years, experts believed that **Paleo-Indians** migrated to America from northeast Asia approximately 10,000 to 12,000 years ago. Scientists believed that they walked into present-day Alaska at a time when sea levels were lower, and the Bering Strait was not covered by water. They speculated that the Paleo-Indians made this journey in pursuit of the animals that they depended upon for food. These people, known as the Clovis Culture, were believed to be the ancestors of all Native American tribal groups.

This theory began to be challenged during the 1980s with the excavation of an

> **The Paleo-Indian Clovis Culture has been traced back to between 10,000 and 8,000 B.C. Archaeologists believe that these people lived beneath rock shelters, inside caves, and in outdoor camps.**

ancient human settlement in Monte Verde, Chile. **Radiocarbon dating** tests performed on pieces of the relics and ruins found at the site indicated that Paleo-Indians had lived there more than 13,000 years ago.

These reconstructed Native American wigwams are made of bark over wooden frames. When Europeans arrived in North America, they found the native peoples living in the same type of dwellings they had used for thousands of years.

Since the discovery at Monte Verde, other early human settlements have been found that indicate Paleo-Indians may have lived in the Americas much earlier than originally thought. Artifacts from the Cactus Hill site in Virginia, for example, have been dated to 17,000 years ago. Another site at Buttermilk Creek in Texas, which was excavated in 2006, has been dated to roughly 16,000 years ago. These discoveries have changed the way anthropologists and archeologists view the early inhabitation of the Americas.

Native Americans living in different areas of the country used different materials to construct their homes, from branches and bark to animal hides and sinew. This bark teepee was made by the native people of California.

Scientists are still unearthing the prehistoric past of the first Americans. No one is 100 percent certain where the first Native American homes were located, as relatively little is known about these **pre-Columbian** people. Much more is known, however, about Native Americans and their homes during the years between 5000 B.C. and A.D. 1900. The chapters that follow will examine some of the more common types of native homes of the Americas. ⑤

This traditional Iroquois longhouse stands Iroquois County, New York. Unlike most dwellings which house one family, a longhouse could be home to up to a dozen families.

2. Dwellings of the Northeast

The Iroquois of the Eastern woodland area lived in longhouses. They called themselves the Haudenosaunee. This word has been interpreted as meaning, "the people of the longhouse."

The length of an Iroquois longhouse depended upon the size of the clan, or family group, that lived within its walls. Some longhouses were hundreds of feet long. Others were less than 50 feet in length. However, the width and height of longhouses seldom varied. Iroquois longhouses were almost always between 20 and 30 feet (6.1 to 9.1 meters) wide. Their roofs were generally 18 to 20 feet (5.5 to 6.1 m) in height.

The Iroquois formed the frames for their long rectangular buildings by securing posts of flexible saplings into the ground. The saplings were bent into arches to frame the longhouse roof. Sheets of birch, elm, or cedar bark were used to cover the entire longhouse frame. These sheets of bark were sewn together and then secured to the frame with strips of the inner bark of the slippery elm or red elm tree.

The typical longhouse was a multifamily dwelling. It had no

> One of the largest longhouses ever built was found in New York State. It measured 400 feet in length. Scientists believe it was built around A.D. 1410.

windows—only a door on each end. The longhouse family's clan symbol was hung over each doorway of the longhouse.

Openings in the roof helped to let light in and let smoke out. During stormy weather, these openings could be closed. The Iroquois used sliding panels to open and close their roof holes.

Interior walls were built out from the two long sidewalls. These were spaced approximately every seven feet (2.1 m) and were placed so as to create a long, open center aisle from one end of the house to the other. Here, every two families shared a fire. Socializing, cooking, and eating took place along this central aisle.

Each individual family that lived within the longhouse had its own section of a raised sleeping platform. These platforms were about one foot (30.5 cm) off the ground. They were covered with bark sheets, reed mats, and furs. Animal-hide curtains were used to provide privacy between the family subdivisions of the sleeping platforms.

Above and below the sleeping platforms were storage shelves. Clothing, corn, dried fish, and meat were hung on pegs placed along the walls. Storage pits were often dug beneath the sleeping platforms of the longhouses. These pits were used to keep food cool and dry.

The Iroquois Confederacy was originally made up of five nations: the Seneca, Mohawk, Oneida, Onondaga, and Cayuga. In 1722, the Tuscaroras were adopted into this league. At this time, the confederacy became known as the Six Nations Confederacy.

Wigwams were the customary homes for the semi-nomadic Algonquian-speaking tribes of the Eastern woodlands area. The Algonquian

A wigwam was built with a frame of tree branches and sticks, then covered with bark or mats woven from tough plants like cattails.

women were responsible for building wigwams. Many Algonquian women could build a traditional birch bark wigwam in one day.

The inner skeletons of seasonally used wigwams could be stripped of their exterior birch bark or cattail mat coverings and left standing in place for future use. The valuable birch bark and cattail mats would be carried from place to place and used again and again. This meant that the Algonquian women often only had to put up the outer shells of their wigwams.

The basic framework of a wigwam consisted of five spruce poles tied together at the top of the wigwam. They were then spread out at the bottom. About a foot from the top of the wigwam, a hoop made out of stripped maple was used to brace the poles. Shorter poles were tied around the circumference of this hoop. Starting at the bottom of the framework, woven cattail mats or birch bark shingles were placed atop the framework. The mats or bark sheets were held in place by

Members of a Dakota Sioux tribe perform a traditional Dog Dance in their village. Their tepees were usually constructed of three or four strong tree branches, which were then wrapped with animal hide to create a conical dwelling.

poles that were laid atop them. A hole was left in the top of the wigwam so that smoke could escape and light could enter. This hole could be covered to keep out the cold, wind, rain, and snow.

Wigwam floors were lined with spruce and fir branches. Woven mats and furs were then placed over the branches. The door was usually covered with an animal pelt or a woven mat. Sometimes, pictures of animals were painted on the wigwams' exteriors.

Twelve to 15 people might fit in the larger, conical-shaped wigwams. If more people needed to be accommodated, then an even longer, two-fireplace wigwam was built. However, wigwams were generally used to house smaller family units rather than extended ones.

Inside the wigwam, the native tribes of the eastern woodlands built raised sleeping platforms around the sides. To the back, or west, of the wigwam was a storage area. In the center was the fireplace, social center, cooking, and dining area. Prairie tribes, who also built wigwams, often slept on grass mats or animal skins placed directly on the ground.

The Dakota summer farm villages featured homes much like the Iroquois longhouses. The fall rice-lake camps were made up of portable bark-sided tepees. Small bark lodges, similar to longhouses, were built in the midst of maple groves. The Dakota Sioux would live in these dwellings during the sugar-making season, which lasted from early March to early May.

The Dakota Sioux, as well as some of the more Northern Algonquian, Iroquois, and Ojibwa tribes also used bark-sided tepees. These portable shelters were used for hunting trips, short journeys, and fair-weather dwellings. The Dakota word "tepee" literally means "dwelling."

To build a bark-sided tepee, Native Americans stuck saplings into the ground in a circular shape. These saplings were leaned into each other and tied together at the top. The poles were then covered with bark sheets.

Lines of holes were made along the edges of the bark siding with an **awl**. The women softened and split tree roots to use as thread. Pieces of bark were sewn together to create long sheets for the sides of the tepee. A waterproof mixture of tree gum and fish oil was used to patch up any gaps around the stitches.

These long strips of bark could be rolled up and carried easily. Lightweight and waterproof, the bark sheets were the perfect siding for the portable tepees of the Northeastern Dakota. Well-made bark sheets were so highly valued that they were often used as a trading commodity. Ƽ

When European explorers arrived in Florida during the 16th century, they found the native Timucua people living in small huts like this one. A Timucua village usually included many huts enclosed by a circular wall.

3 Homes in the Southeast

Chickee is the Seminole word for "house." The Seminoles of North Florida built log cabin-type homes until the Indian Removal Act of 1830 went into effect. Their log cabins were permanent two-story structures. The sleeping quarters were usually upstairs.

In response to the Indian Removal Act of 1830, the Seminoles went into hiding. It was then that they began building and perfecting the chickee. Tracked and hunted by U.S. troops, the Seminoles needed shelter that was quick and easy to construct. The Seminole also needed housing that they could destroy or abandon abruptly. This would allow them to cover their tracks from the U.S. troops pursuing them. Their new housing also had to be suitable for life in the swamps, **everglades**, and wetlands of Florida.

The Seminoles built their chickees using cypress logs and palm thatch leaves. The cypress logs were pushed into the ground. The palm thatch leaves were woven together with vines to create a roof for the structure. Chickees were always raised off the ground to protect the sleeping Seminole inside from poisonous snakes and other dangerous wetland creatures.

The chickee had no walls. It was an open-air structure with only a thatched roof. At first, the Seminoles only made single-level chickees.

This level, raised platform was used primarily as a sleeping area. Eventually, the Seminoles began to build chickees that were two stories high. The upper level was used as a sleeping or living area. The lower level served as a storage area or as a sleeping and living area for larger families.

The Muskoke, or Creek, built their homes out of saplings, clay, dried grass, and cypress bark. They built the walls by setting a string of slender poles into the ground. Saplings were split and woven between these posts. The frames of the houses were then covered with clay and dried grasses. The doors were low and narrow.

The roofs of these dwellings were made much like the walls. Split saplings were woven together. However, unlike the clay and dried-grass–covered walls, the roofs were covered with cypress bark. The roofs were supported by walls, rafters, and interior posts and would always have one smoke hole to provide ventilation.

The Cherokee built what are known as **wattle and daub** houses. First, they would

> Three poles usually stood within Muskoke plazas. The tallest pole was used for a traditional pole ball game called chunkey. The other two were used to display scalps and other souvenirs taken in battles. In addition, prisoners were often tied to these two war poles.

construct rounded outer frameworks from interwoven branches. Next, the frameworks were plastered with mud. Finally, the dwellings were topped with thatched or cane mat roofs.

Another common style of dwelling was the wattle and daub hut. Made mostly from tree trunks and branches (wattle), the house was smeared with mud (daub) to seal and insulate it.

A clay fireplace was sometimes built in the center of the dirt floor. Smoke rose up through the center of the house and then out of a hole in the roof. These dwellings were sometimes built partially underground to help keep the Cherokee cool during the hot Southeastern summers.

The Chickasaw used two different seasonal types of shelters. A Chickasaw summer home was rectangular in shape, and the roof was

This drawing shows the style of Native American villages the earliest European explorers found when they arrived in Florida. The wall around the village was built to protect the inhabitants from invaders and wild animals.

peaked, or triangular. These summer houses were approximately 12 feet (3.7 m) wide and 25 feet (7.6 m) long.

The Chickasaw often built porches and balconies for their homes. These were used for cooking and socializing. They may also have been used for sleeping when the weather was unbearably hot.

The winter houses of the Chickasaw were rounded wattle and daub buildings, much like those of the Cherokee. They were smaller than the Chickasaw summer lodges. They protected their inhabitants from the elements by featuring living and sleeping quarters that were built down into the earth.

The Choctaw built wattle and daub or mud-and-bark cabins with

The Choctaw once lived in what is now Mississippi and western Alabama. They called themselves the "Chata Hapia Hoke." "Chata" is thought to be a Choctaw version of the Spanish word "chato," which means "flat." The Choctaw were known to practice the Native American custom of flattening the heads of their children. They believed that flat heads would allow their children to have sharp, clear vision.

thatched roofs of cane, reeds, cattails, and straw. The Choctaw occasionally covered sapling frameworks with animal hides, dried grasses, woven mats, or bark. They sometimes even made walls out of crushed seashells and mud.

The Arawak referred to themselves as Taino, or "good people." These pre-Columbian people lived throughout the Caribbean. Taino villages were called yucayeques.

Large groups of Taino families lived in *bohios.* One *bohio* might house from 10 to 15 Taino men, as well as their entire families. It was not uncommon for a *bohio* to serve as the home of up to 100 Taino people.

These houses were quite large. A traditional Taino family's *bohio* was a circular building made of poles covered with woven straw, cane plants, palm tree stems, and palm leaves. The roof of a *bohio* was cone-shaped.

The *caney,* or chief's home, was even larger than a *bohio*. It was rectangular, rather than circular. The chief's home might even have a small porch extending from one end of his family *caney.* ⑤

23

The word "hammock" comes from the Arawak word *hamaca*. A *hamaca* was a hanging bed made of twisted cotton strings or fibers harvested from the Maguey plant.

The teepee was the traditional home of Native Americans
who lived on the Great Plains.

4 Homes of the West and Southwest

The basic design of the tepee used on the Great Plains differed only in minor ways from tribe to tribe. The Hidatsa, Crow, and Blackfoot used a four-pole base for their tepees. The Arapaho, Cheyenne, Kiowa, and Sioux used a three-pole base for their tepees. Each tribe, and each family within those tribes, adorned their tepees in their own personal manner. The decorations on the outside of a tepee were generally of a spiritual nature. The paintings on the inside of a tepee often told the family's or tribe's history.

The people of the Plains needed dwellings that could be adapted to the requirements of an **itinerant** lifestyle. These homes had to be easy to put up, take down, and transport from camp to camp. The tepee had all of these necessary qualities and more.

A tepee provides warm shelter in the winter and cool shelter in the summer. When properly smoked, tepee coverings can endure heavy rains and snowstorms. When properly set up, a tepee is able to stand up against severe winds and weather.

Women of the Plains tribes usually set up their family's tepees. Tepees were often considered to be the property of the women of the tribes and family units.

To set up a tepee, three or four base poles are usually made from the wood of the lodge-pole pine tree. These poles are tied together with a piece of animal sinew or thin strips of rawhide. The poles are then raised into a tripod or four-pod foundation. More lodge-pole pine poles are braced around the base to form the outer skeleton of the tepee. The poles are positioned so that the tepee is steeper in the back than it is in the front. This helps the tepee to withstand fierce winds.

The stories and symbols of humans and animals were illustrated around the middle section of the outer sides of the tepee. The painted designs around the bottom of the tepee cover symbolized Mother Earth. The tops of tepees were painted to honor Father Sky.

Usually from 12 to 17 poles were used in addition to the tripod or four-pod base of a tepee. The last pole to be set up was a pole at the back of the tepee. This pole was used to raise the buffalo hide tepee cover, which was tied to it. Sometimes, a pocket was sewn into the hide and the top of the back pole was slipped into this pocket. As it was raised, it pulled the tepee cover up with it.

Buffalo hides were used to make tepee coverings. The hides had to be scraped to remove any flesh from them. Next, the women removed all of the hair from the hides and then tanned and dried them. When the hides were dried, they were ready to be sewn together for use as a tepee covering. Ten to 15 buffalo hides might be used for a single tepee covering.

Members of the Atsina tribe move their home to a
new settlement. The second and third horses are each
pulling travois made from the poles of the family's
teepee. The travois enabled the Native Americans of
the Great Plains to easily move their belongings as
they shifted their camps with the herds of buffalo.

NATIVE AMERICAN LIFE

When setting up a tepee, the hide covering was unfolded and stretched

out from the back. It was then pulled around the sides. At the front, or

eastern, side of the tepee, it was secured above the doorway with wooden

stakes or pins. The cover was then stretched and smoothed out carefully.

The women would check to make sure it was wrapped tightly around

Some of the early Native American tribes that lived in earth lodges included the Mandan, Hidatsa, and Pawnee. Their homes were often built into a hill for permanence and warmth.

the framework of the tepee. When it was correctly shaped and stretched, the bottom edge was fastened to the ground with stakes.

Smoke flaps at the top were controlled by two long poles on either side of the outside of the tepee. The flaps helped provide the right amount of ventilation for the fire. They could be opened or closed depending on the weather conditions.

Most tepees had an inner buffalo-hide covering that started a few feet from the top of the tepee and reached almost all the way to the ground. This covering served as additional protection from water leakage due to heavy rains or snows. The covering was also used as an extra barrier against cold drafts and helped to provide insulation from the weather conditions outside the tepee.

The basic residence of the Hidatsa, Mandan, and other upper-Missouri tribes was the earth lodge. These tribes did occasionally use tepees for hunting or gathering camps. However, they most often made their homes out of wood and clay.

The rudimentary frame of the earth lodge was composed of four large cottonwood logs set perpendicularly into the ground. Substantial wooden crossbeams were connected to each other at the top and were constructed into a square. Smaller logs were placed vertically in a circular shape around this frame.

Long beams were arranged between the inner square and the outer circle. These were used to support the roof. Beams that extended from the outer circle to the ground formed the walls. Small branches were placed over the main rafters. The earth lodge was then layered with willow branches, grasses, and sod. A layer of clay was packed onto the outer roof to waterproof the shelter.

The fire was built in the center of the lodge. Seats were arranged in a semicircle around the fire. The opening of the semicircle would be opposite the family's sacred place. Here, sacred bundles were kept.

Beds were situated around the circumference of the earth lodge. These beds often had four posts. Hides or woven blankets were hung from these posts to provide privacy.

In parts of California and the area known as the Great Basin, simple brush huts were commonly constructed. These huts featured a willow

29

NATIVE AMERICAN LIFE

The Navajo traveled according to the seasons, moving to areas that would provide the best planting, hunting, and weather during that time of the year. Navajo families usually had a winter and a summer home. The log hogan pictured here would have been the family's primary home.

framework, which was covered with **tule**, brush, or grass mats.

Approximately 10 to 15 holes were dug in a circular shape. Long willow branches were stuck into these holes. The willow branches were generally 10 feet (3 m) tall, but sometimes could be even taller. Next, supple green willow branches were tied about two feet up (0.6 m) from the bottoms of the willows that had been placed into the earth.

This was done so as to pull the first willow branches in toward the center of the structure.

Another two feet (0.6 m) up from the first green willow ties, additional willows were tied around the circular framework. These branches were used to pull the framework into the shape of a dome. A smoke hole was left in the center of the dome's roof.

Walls were woven mats made from grasses or tule tied into place around the dome's frame. An area facing east was left open for a doorway. Oftentimes, these doorways were covered with mats that could be easily removed and replaced upon entering or exiting the huts.

Navajo hogans were constructed according to traditional spiritual instructions. They were built of wood and mud and the entrance always faced the east. The first traditional hogans were round, in honor of the sun and the circular patterns of life.

Men would traditionally sit in the southern area of the hogan. Women would sit to the north, across from the men. Guests would be seated in the western section of the hogan.

Two traditional types of hogans were referred to as being male or female. Ceremonies were usually held in male hogans. The male hogan is a place where the tribe meets with enemies or tries to rid sick tribal members of their diseases. This practice avoided bringing enemies or disease into a family dwelling. The female hogan is where the family slept and ate. It was kept as a safe place for the family, particularly the women and children.

A well-built hogan has thick earthen walls, which keep it cool during the summer and warm during the winter. Many, but not all, hogans were built down into the earth. Their construction started with the digging of a large pit. Then poles approximately five feet (1.5 m) in length were used to line the walls of the pit. There were no windows built into the outside walls. The framework for the hogan's ceiling consisted of poles laid on each other in a circular fashion.

The four major supporting logs of the hogan were placed in honor of the Native American deities of the east, west, north, and south. Beneath the hogan, supporting the entrance, were two large stone slabs buried deeply into the ground. Light was able to enter the hogan through an opening at the top of the ceiling. The opening was usually about two feet square.

White corn meal was, and still is, often rubbed onto the main beams of the structure. This is part of a ceremony that a family may choose to use in order to bless a new hogan. Often, a Navajo spiritual leader would be called in to perform a Blessingway Ceremony when a new hogan was built. This practice is still observed today.

The Anasazi lived in the Southwest American and Northern Mexican desert region roughly 2,000 years ago. Anthropologists and archeologists believe that they are the ancestors of the Hopi, the Zuñi, and the Pueblo. The Anasazi lived in **pit houses** during the early days of the Basket Maker Era.

Then, during the latter days of the Basket Maker Era and the early days of the Pueblo Era, they began to build and live in their famous

The Pueblo people of the Southwest are descendents
of the Anasazi tribe, who occupied the Mesa Verde
area of Colorado. Their ancient apartment-like cliff
dwellings can still be seen today.

cliff dwellings. Many of these ancient homes can still be seen today nestled atop the mesas and along the mountain faces of the Southwest, and many Hopi still live in pueblo settlements.

The building material that they used during the Pueblo Era was a mix of clay, sand, and straw formed into bricks. These were then baked in the hot desert sun until they hardened.

The region's violent winds and rains continually **eroded** the pueblo walls. To combat this erosion, the women would make a mud-based plaster. This was put onto the walls and smoothed out by hand at least once a year.

Some Pueblo villages were built atop **mesas**. Others were built right into the sides of mountains. These flat-roofed compartmental homes were often stacked, one atop another, from three to five stories high.

The flat roof of the pueblo served many purposes. It could be used as a place to dry **venison**. Scouts could survey the land for signs of approaching enemies from these heights. During the summer harvest and winter animal dances, these flat roofs became convenient seating areas for those villagers who wanted to watch these important spiritual festivities.

Kivas were the sacred sites for many of the Anasazi and Pueblo cultures' religious ceremonies and spiritual rituals. The Chaco Anasazi, in particular, built large underground kivas. Their kivas were often over 50 feet (15.2 m) in diameter and 10 feet (3 m) tall.

The kiva is a circular-shaped room, completely or partially underground. Pueblo boys and men entered a kiva by climbing down a ladder that led them into a central opening in the kiva's flat roof. It is believed that only men and boys were allowed to enter a village kiva.

Apache families often lived in wickiups built by mothers and their daughters. A wickiup was a small, rounded, roofed hut. These brush lodges provided their occupants with fresh air, shade, and protection from the elements during the summer. The entrance was traditionally placed facing toward the northeast or east. This allowed the morning sun to shine into the wickiup entrance. It also helped to shield the occupants from the winds that generally swept across the area from west to east.

When building a wickiup, first a level spot had to be found. An eight-foot (2.4 m) circle was drawn in the dirt where the wickiup was to be built. Then the women dug a small trench along the circular outline.

Thin poles of oak or willow were placed vertically into the trench. These poles were used to make the wickiup's frame. Strands of a rope-like material made from the yucca plant were used to tie the tops of the poles together.

The typical wickiup was only four to six feet (1.2 to 1.8 m) high at its highest point. An opening was left at the top of the hut, allowing light to filter into the wickiup. It also allowed smoke from the fire to be ventilated up and out of the wickiup. ⑤

35

NATIVE AMERICAN LIFE

The Inuit word "igloo" actually means any type of dwelling. This igloo was made of hard-packed blocks of snow, which were cut into regular shapes and stacked. An Inuit man could usually build a home this size in about an hour.

5 Living Quarters in the Far North

Warm shelter was important in the Arctic and subarctic regions of North America. One type of home was the sod dwelling. These were shaped like small hills. From a distance, they might appear to be nothing more than small mounds jutting out of the **tundra** or **taiga**.

The houses were built using a frame composed of driftwood or whale jaw and rib bones. The frames were then covered with sod. In the winter months, snow was often piled around the sod to add an extra layer of insulation to the dwelling. These houses were built so that the occupants walked down into them through a small doorway on one side. For the most part, the living space was underground.

A small sod house featured one large room that was used for both sleeping and eating. A large sod house might have two rooms connected by a narrow passageway. In this case, the outer room was used for cooking, storing supplies, and perhaps for visiting. The inner room would have been used as a sleeping area.

Sod dwellings allowed light to enter through holes that were cut into the ceiling. These holes were concealed with covers made from animal intestines. Smoke from fires and oil lamps was able to drift out through these holes. Oils from various animals were used to make oil lamps that helped provide light in these dark subterranean sod homes.

To build a snow dome, first a clearing about 10 to 20 feet (3 to 6.1 m) wide was opened in the snow and the ground was leveled. Next, blocks of ice approximately two feet by two feet by four inches were shaped and cut. These blocks were placed along the edges of the circular clearing. The next rows of ice blocks were placed so that they leaned closer and closer in towards the top of the snow dome. The person who was stacking the ice blocks did so from the area that would soon be the snow dome's interior. Another person stood outside of the ice wall and patted it down with snow. The snow helped to hold the ice blocks together and added extra insulation to the structure. When the dome was completed, a small door was cut into the bottom of one of the walls. These doors were usually placed about one to three feet from the ground.

Snow domes were temporary dwellings. They were used as emergency shelters for hunters and travelers who were caught in the frigid weather of the Arctic and subarctic territories. It is believed that only the people of the Thule Culture ever really used snow domes as more than a temporary shelter. These people also used underground sod dwellings as well as skin tents that were stretched across frames made from animal bones.

The Aleuts lived along the coast of the Alaska Peninsula. Their homes were a lot like the sod houses of the Inuit people. The Aleut called their houses *barabaras*.

An entire Aleut village might inhabit a single *barabaras*. The Aleut were known to build *barabaras* over 200 feet (61 m) long and 30 feet (9.1 m) wide. A large Aleut dwelling of this type might be home to more than 100 people. The average Aleut home, however, was approximately 20 by 36 feet (9.1 to 11 m). A home of this size would provide shelter for up to approximately 50 people.

During the summer, the people of the Arctic and subarctic regions used many forms of temporary shelters. Some lived in conical-shaped caribou-skin tents that were much like the Plains tepees. Large rocks were used to hold down the edges of these skin tents. The reason rocks were used instead of wooden stakes was because wood was hard to come by for many of the people of the Arctic and subarctic regions.

The word "igloo," which is used to mean "snow dome" by many people, really just means "house" or "home" in the Inuit language. One Inuit way of spelling igloo is "iglu."

In the winter, the Tanaina employed dwellings made of logs and sod that were built into the earth. Simple summer huts were built for use during the salmon runs. These huts were often small log buildings that doubled as smokehouses for drying fish.

The Slavey constructed summer shelters that were simple brush-covered tepees. In the winter, they built sturdier rectangular huts. They formed these huts using spruce poles and branches. If cottonwood or birch trees were available, the Slavey would use these trees as building supplies also.

39

NATIVE AMERICAN LIFE

Haida plank houses were, in some ways, similar to the Iroquois longhouses of the Northeast woodlands area. The Northwest coastal Haida built their houses using long cedar planks. The Haida obtained these planks by splitting the trunks of tall cedar trees.

A standard Haida plank house might measure anywhere from 50 to 100 feet (15.2 to 30.5 m) in length. Many of these houses were between 15 and 25 feet (4.6 and 7.6 m) in width. Haida homes needed to be quite large, as they were often the residences of several families. Occasionally, an entire Haida village shared a single plank house.

The roof of a Haida house was pitched, or angled. This helped to keep snow from building up on the roof and collapsing it. An **adze** was used to trim the timbers that supported the roof beams, which in turn supported the roof.

The walls were constructed using a series of vertical cedar boards secured between horizontal timbers. There were no windows in the walls of these homes, and the floors were earthen. The women often made floor coverings out of woven rush mats, which provided the inhabitants with an extra layer of insulation from the cold ground.

Each family had its own living space between its sleeping quarters and fire pit. A family's sleeping area started at the plank house wall and extended inward toward the fire pit. Beds were made out of mats woven from beaten cedar bark or rushes. Cedar bark was also combined with animal fur to create finely woven blankets.

In Tlingit society, there were three classes: nobles, commoners, and slaves. Tlingit slaves were often members of other tribes or

The Haida society had three levels: aristocrats, commoners, and slaves. This model of a Haida chief's house was elaborately decorated and features a carefully carved totem pole, an architectural trait for which the culture was known.

Traditional designs cover the
exterior of a Tlingit clan house
in Alaska. The Tlingit were
closely related to the Haida,
and they were also recognized
for their skill in carving and
ornamentation.

bands who had been kidnapped from neighboring villages. Sometimes, too, they were Tlingit enemies who had been captured during battle. Each of these three classes had their own area of a Tlingit house.

A Tlingit house was a large rectangle with cedar planks set along the sides. A low-sloping, peaked roof topped it. Four decorated corner posts and a center **ridge beam** held up the roof.

Inside, the floor was dug down so the sides of the house could hold two or more levels of benches. There was a low platform where people sat. A higher platform was divided by wooden partitions into sleeping compartments.

At the rear of each house, in front of or inside its storeroom for sacred treasures, lived members of the nobility. Along the sides lived families of commoners. Slaves slept beside the oval front door.

Along the sides of the house where they lived, families kept their own open fires for cooking and heating. In the middle, however, was a large public hearth. This hearth was used to cook meals for the nobles or for guests attending a celebration.

The Interior Salish often built their sunken roundhouse villages close to a river. Rivers were a source of fish and of fresh drinking water. They provided the Salish with a place to wash their belongings and bathe. Rivers were also the chief means of Salish transportation.

Construction of a Salish underground roundhouse began with the digging of a round or oval hole. These pits were usually about six feet deep and were often between 15 and 40 feet (4.6 and 12.1 m) wide.

43

NATIVE AMERICAN LIFE

Once the pit for the roundhouse was dug, the floor was covered with several layers of spruce boughs. Next, a pointed, tapering framework of poles was erected. This framework served as the foundation for the roundhouse's roof.

The framework was insulated with a heavy layer of spruce boughs. Additional poles were added to fill in any gaps in the roof. Finally, the soil that had been dug out to make the roundhouse pit was used to cover the dwelling.

An opening approximately four feet (1.2 m) square was left in the roof and used as a doorway. The Salish kept a ladder, consisting of a series of simple steps carved into a log, in the doorway. The bottom of the ladder was pushed into the interior floor of the roundhouse. The top of the ladder protruded out of the hole in the roof. Entering and exiting a Salish roundhouse could be a rather smoky affair, as the doorway doubled as a smoke hole.

Salish roundhouses were often home to several families. Each family had its own sleeping quarters. The fire was centrally located so that it provided heat and light as evenly as possible to all areas of the round house. The central location ensured that it was also easily shared for cooking.

In the summer, the Salish lived above ground. They often built rounded rectangular or funnel-shaped lodges covered with rush mats. These bulrush longhouses were typically covered with woven tule mats. The Cayuse also often utilized bulrush or tule longhouses for both summer and winter dwellings.

The frame for this type of longhouse was built using lodge poles made from straight pine trees. These poles were fitted together to form a strong frame. A ridgeline consisting of two or more poles was built into the structure of the roof. The ridgeline lent support and strength to the roof of the longhouse. Once the ridgeline was in place, the tule mat coverings were added.

It was normal for several families to live together in one bulrush longhouse. To accommodate the comings and goings of these families, entrances were built along the sides. Each family had its own area in the bulrush longhouse. Much like the Iroquois, the Northwestern tribes who lived in bulrush longhouses set their many cooking and heating fires in a central aisle spaced about eight to 10 feet (2.4 to 3 m) apart.

Bulrush lodges were built so that they would be relatively easy to keep warm and cozy in the winter as well as relatively easy to keep cool in the summer. The tules used in the woven mat coverings adapted perfectly to all types of weather. When it rained, the tules swelled. As they swelled, the mats became tighter and harder for rain to penetrate. On hot arid days, the tules shrank. This helped to lower the temperature inside the bulrush lodge during the summer months. More air was able to breeze through the tule mats, creating a sort of as-needed air conditioning system. ☉

45

NATIVE AMERICAN LIFE

The typical home of a Mayan family in Belize.
Many of the indigenous people of Central America
continue to observe traditional ways, depending on
nearby forests and rivers for survival. Foreign logging
companies threaten both the rainforests and the
traditional lifestyle of native people.

Central and South American Homes

The warm regions of Mexico and Central America were home to several complex Native American civilizations. One of the most advanced of these civilizations was that of the Maya, who flourished from about 400 B.C. until A.D. 900. During this period the Maya built many large cities, featuring enormous stone pyramids and palaces that are still standing today. Pre-Columbian Mayan homes ranged from the complicated palace buildings of the priests and ruling class to the simple thatched-roof wooden walled or wattle-and-daub thatched roof huts of the common class.

Many Mayans still live in isolated areas of the Central American rainforest. The homes of these rural Mayans are much like those of their ancestors from the ancient Mayan common class. Scattered throughout the northern Yucatán region and parts of the highlands in Guatemala, these residents of the rainforest live a traditional Mayan lifestyle that has not changed much over the years.

Archeological digs in various parts of Central and South America have turned up remnants from the homes of Mayan commoners, some of which date back to 1,000 B.C. These homes bear a remarkable resemblance to the huts of modern-day rural Mayans. For example, many of these ancient huts were made with wattle-and-daub walls. They were oval in shape and had thatched roofs. Palmetto fronds were used then, as now, as a basic material for these thatched roofs.

The Garifuna and Miskito people of Nicaragua live in bamboo and grass huts that are referred to as *palapas*. The roofs of these huts are made from palms or dried grasses. These palm fronds or grasses are securely tied with vines to ridgepoles.

The frames of these *palapas* are made from the wood of the mangrove tree. One commonly held belief is that the best palapas frames are made from mangrove trees that have been harvested during a full moon. These trees must then be soaked for three days prior to use in hut building.

The De'áruwa of South America live in communal family settlements. A settlement consists of a group of homes called *churuatas*. The *churuata* is bell-shaped with a pointed, conical roof. The roof of a *churata* is made from palm leaves. Clay, or sometimes wood, may be used to construct the walls. Internal rafters are positioned in a circular pattern to support the *churata*'s frame.

Because the weather of Central and South America was often warm and mild, families would need only to build grass or reed huts to keep out wind and rain. The huts were simple to build and plain in appearance, because they were not intended to be permanent dwellings.

During the high point of Mayan civilization, amazing stone temples and pyramids were built. These Mayan ruins overlook the ocean at Tulum, Mexico.

The interior of a *churata* is open, without dividing walls. Every family has its own area within the *churata*. The central area is where the De'áruwa gather to perform rituals, make crafts, and entertain guests.

In Brazil, the huts of a Waiãpi village are scattered across the land in a seemingly random pattern. Actually, they are carefully spaced in an effort to make the most out of the available terrain. The Waiãpi are farmers, hunters, and gatherers.

Each hut is home to a family, or a small extended family, of between four to seven people. Not only do the people need to find room for their huts, but land must also be set aside for a communal gathering area, which is used for social activities and ceremonial rituals.

Traditional huts are thatched-roof buildings built on wooden pillars. Ubim leaves and black straw are used as roofing materials. The huts are generally raised about six feet off the ground. The occupants of these homes climb up wooden ladders to enter them.

Besides the homes, all villages also have one to three or more huts serving as kitchens with hearths and all tools necessary for **cassava** processing. These buildings serve several families, and mothers and daughters meet together to prepare food in them.

The Yanomamo live in the tropical rainforests of Brazil and Venezuela. They are farmers and hunter-gatherers. Yanomamo families live in a house called a *shabono*.

A *shabono* is basically a large, circular lean-to. Each *shabono* has a roof and a back wall. There are no front or side walls. A *shabono* is primarily a place for the Yanomamo to seek shelter from the rain and hang their hammocks. The Yanomamo sit, sleep, and rest in hammocks that hang down from their roofs. Another area beneath the thatched *shabono* roof is the cooking and eating area. Centrally located, this is also a place for ceremonial dances and community get-togethers.

The roof of a *shabono* is thatched. Most *shabono* roofs last from three to five years. After that, the thatched roofs begin to rot due to the hot, moist weather of the rainforest. When this happens, rodents begin to infest first the *shabono* roofs and then the entire village. At this point, the Yanomamo either move and build an entirely new village or destroy their old *shabonos* and build new ones in a nearby location. Ƨ

51

NATIVE AMERICAN LIFE

Pueblo homes had several stories and
many rooms, much like modern
apartments. Each family had only one
room. Early Pueblo settlements were built
in caves high in canyon walls or on the
ledges of cliffs. Later communities were
built in valleys and on mesas, like the Taos
Pueblo in New Mexico, shown here.

7 Conclusion

Native American homes of the past were, much like their owners, unique and well suited to a lifestyle that honored and depended upon the lands, seas, and animals of the American continents. The great palaces of the Mayan people now shelter memories of the past. Many of the adobe apartment houses of the Pueblo people are now home only to the winds, sands, and extreme temperatures of the desert. The remains of abandoned Inuit sod houses shield aging walrus skulls and whale bones from the harsh Arctic winds.

These places were once home to Native American families. Women prepared meals for their husbands and children. Men told stories of hunting and farming skills. Children played happily, slept soundly, and ate heartily. Sacred ceremonies were held within their walls. New generations were born beneath their roofs. The feet of dancers, hunters, gatherers, farmers, and warriors graced their floors. Spirits were honored around their fires.

Some traditional Native American homes are now kept as spirit houses. Some people believe that the spirits of those who lived in these places long ago still linger in them. Others believe that the spirits of the Earth reside in these humble homes. Aging traditional Native

A Navajo woman weaves in her hogan on the Hopi Reservation. Her home is a traditional small octagonal dirt and wood dwelling without plumbing or electricity in the arid desert of Arizona.

American homes and their ruins are still used for honoring the spirits through Native American religious ceremonies. The shelters are symbols of cultures that have evolved and survived.

> From 8000 to 500 B.C., the Archaic Era-people stalked game animals, fished, and gathered edible plants. Their homes were tent-like dwellings constructed of timber frames wrapped with tree bark or animal pelts.

In the past, the environmental surroundings and lifestyle issues of each tribe constantly challenged Native American ingenuity and architectural know–how. Native Americans learned to use the natural resources most available to them when building their homes. They also learned to build homes that could be efficiently heated or cooled.

However, Native Americans today are seeking shelter from poor housing conditions. In many places throughout the United States, Mexico, Central, and South America, Native Americans live in substandard contemporary housing and often live without running water or proper bathroom plumbing. In some of these areas, electricity is not even available.

The United States' government, the governments of Mexico and various Central and South American nations, and many various American Native Tribal Associations are working diligently to assure that Native Americans everywhere are provided adequate housing. Much has been done to help change these conditions, but there is still much more to do. §

55

NATIVE AMERICAN LIFE

CHRONOLOGY

Before 10,000 B.C. Paleo-Indians migrate from parts of Asia and begin settling throughout the Americas.

10,000–5000 B.C. Medicine-wheel spiritual sites are built in the Great Basin region.

6000–5000 B.C. The subarctic regions are settled as the climate begins to warm with the waning of the last Ice Age.

5000–3000 B.C. Earliest-known organized Native American settlements are built in the Southeast.

1400 B.C.–A.D. 1500 Northeastern woodland cultures rise and prosper.

A.D. 300–900 Maya civilization reaches its highest point; Native Americans begin settling in the Plains region and migrating with the buffalo herds and the seasons of the year.

1400–1521 The Aztecs dominate Mesoamerica.

1492–1502 Columbus explores the West Indies and Central America.

1740–1780 European wars in the Northeast severely affect lifestyles of Native Americans in this region.

1760–1848 Growing Spanish influence in and around California begins to have impact on the lives of Native Americans in this region; missionaries begin attempts to "civilize" and "Christianize" Native Americans of this area.

1830 Congress passes the Indian Removal Act, calling for Native Americans living east of the Mississippi River to be moved to a government-established Indian Territory located in what is present-day Oklahoma.

1838 Cherokee are forced to move from the Southeast to Oklahoma on the "Trail of Tears."

1887 The Dawes/General Allotment Act divides reservations into 80- and 160-acre tracts; these land parcels are to be owned by individual Native Americans.

1952 The Federal Relocation Policy is passed; this policy seeks to terminate all government services for Native Americans, negate treaty agreements, and relocate Native Americans from reservations to inner cities.

1971 Congress passes the Alaska Native Claims Settlement Act.

1972 "Trail of Broken Treaties" organized by AIM results in a weeklong occupation of the Bureau of Indian Affairs headquarters in Washington, D.C.

1992 This year marks the 500th anniversary of Columbus' entry to the West Indies, prompting many Native American artists to create artwork expressing their feelings about Columbus and subsequent Europeans and their effects upon the Native American culture.

2013 Recent census figures indicate there are more than 5.2 million Native Americans living in the United States and Canada.

GLOSSARY

adze a tool used primarily for dressing and squaring large timbers; an adze is similar to an axe, but has its cutting edge placed at a right angle to the handle.

anthropologist a scientist who studies humans and the evolution of the human species.

archaeologist a scientist who studies history through the examination of ancient ruins and artifacts.

awl a pointed tool used for poking holes in leather and other tough materials.

cassava a type of melon.

erode to wear away, usually by wind or water.

everglade a stretch of marshy grassland usually covered with water for at least part of the year.

itinerant traveling from place to place.

mesa an isolated, relatively flat-topped natural elevation.

Paleo-Indians Stone Age inhabitants of the Americas.

pit house semi-underground home that was round, square, oval, or rectangular and was constructed using a combination of natural resources.

pre-Columbian the period of American history before Columbus began exploring the West Indies and Caribbean.

radiocarbon dating a means of dating ancient materials in which the amount of the radioactive isotope, carbon 14, is measured.

ridge beam a beam placed horizontally along the peak of a roof to provide support.

taiga a moist subarctic forest dominated by conifers that begins where the tundra ends.

tule a reed or bulrush used to make huts and mats.

tundra a level or rolling treeless plain that is characteristic of Arctic and subarctic regions.

venison deer meat.

wattle and daub mud or clay plaster used to cover a framework of poles that are entwined with branches and vines to build the walls of a dwelling.

FURTHER READING

Barnes, Ian. *Historical Atlas of Native Americans*. London: Cartographica Press, 2009.

Hoffman, Elizabeth DeLaney. *American Indians and Popular Culture*. 2 vols. Santa Barbara, Calif.: ABC-CLIO, 2012.

Johnson, Michael, and Richard Hook. *Encyclopedia of Native Tribes of North America*. Buffalo, N.Y.: Firefly Books, 2007.

Oberg, Michael Leroy. *Native America: A History*. Malden, U.K.: Blackwell Publishing, 2010.

Waldman, Carl. *Encyclopedia of Native American Tribes*. New York: Facts on File, 2006.

Williams, Colleen Madonna Flood. *Native American Family Life*. Philadelphia: Mason Crest Publishers, 2014.

NATIVE AMERICAN LIFE

INTERNET RESOURCES

http://www.csulb.edu/colleges/cla/departments/americanindianstudies/faculty/trj
Website of the American Indian Studies program at California State University, Long Beach, which is chaired by Professor Troy Johnson. The site presents unique artwork, photographs, video, and sound recordings that accurately reflect the rich history and culture of Native Americans.

http://inquiryunlimited.org/timelines/histNatAm.html
The Native American Timeline website includes timeframes, topics, resources, and a discussion forum for all sorts of information pertaining to Native Americans.

http://www.nativeweb.org/resources
This website features a collection of resources and links to informative Native American Web sites.

http://www.native-languages.org/houses.htm
This site includes information about many different types of Native American dwellings.

www.nativepeoples.com
This is the website for Native People's Arts and Lifeways magazine. It contains information on all sorts of issues pertaining to native peoples.

Publisher's Note: The websites listed on this page were active at the time of publication. The publisher is not responsible for websites that have changed their address or discontinued operation since the date of publication. The publisher reviews and updates the websites each time the book is reprinted.

INDEX

NATIVE AMERICAN LIFE

63

PICTURE CREDITS

NATIVE AMERICAN LIFE

CONTRIBUTORS

Dr. Troy Johnson is chairman of the American Indian Studies program at California State University, Long Beach, California. He is an internationally published author and is the author, co-author, or editor of twenty books, including *Wisdom Spirits: American Indian Prophets, Revitalization Movements, and Cultural Survival* (University of Nebraska Press, 2012); *The Indians of Eastern Texas and The Fredonia Revolution of 1828* (Edwin Mellen Press, 2011); and *The American Indian Red Power Movement: Alcatraz to Wounded Knee* (University of Nebraska Press, 2008). He has published numerous scholarly articles, has spoken at conferences across the United States, and is a member of the editorial board of the journals *American Indian Culture and Research and The History Teacher.* Dr. Johnson has served as president of the Society of History Education since 2001. He has won awards for his permanent exhibit at Alcatraz Island; he also was named Most Valuable Professor of the Year by California State University, Long Beach, in 1997 and again in 2006. He served as associate director and historical consultant on the award-winning PBS documentary film *Alcatraz Is Not an Island* (1999). Dr. Johnson lives in Long Beach, California.

Colleen Madonna Flood Williams holds a bachelor's degree in elementary education, with a minor in art. She lives with her beloved husband Paul, and son, Dillon, in Soldotna, Alaska. She is the author of several other educational children's books for Mason Crest Publishers.